The Notebook

2 | Minister Onedia and Hillary

The Notebook
for the
Christian Teen

The Notebook

4 | Minister Onedia and Hillary

The Notebook
for the
Christian Teen

By
Minister Onedia N. Gage
with
Hillary Nicole

The Notebook

Other Books by Onedia N. Gage, M. Ed., MBA

Are You Ready for 9th Grade . . . Again? A Family's Guide to Success

As We Grow Together Daily Devotional for Expectant Couples

As We Grow Together Prayer Journal for Expectant Couples

The Blue Print: Poetry for the Soul

From Two to One: The Notebook for the Christian Couple

In Her Own Words: The Notebook for the Christian Woman

In Purple Ink: Poetry for the Spirit

Living a Whole Life: Sermons which Prompt, Provoke and Promote Life

Love Letters to God from a Teenage Girl

The Measure of a Woman: The Details of Her Soul

The Notebook: For Me, About Me, By Me

On This Journey Daily Devotional for Young People

On This Journey Prayer Journal for Young People

One Day More Than We Deserve Daily Devotional for the Growing Christian

One Day More Than We Deserve Prayer Journal for the Growing Christian

Promises, Promises: A Christian Novel

Tools for These Times: Timely Sermons for Uncertain Times

With An Anointed Voice: The Power of Prayer

Yielded and Submitted: A Woman's Journey for a Life Dedicated to God

Yielded and Submitted: A Woman's Journey for a Life Dedicated to God Prayers and Journal

Yielded and Submitted: A Woman's Journey for a Life Dedicated to God An Intimate Study

The Notebook

Library of Congress

The Notebook
For the Christian Teen

All Rights Reserved © 2014

Onedia N. Gage

Hillary Nicole

No part of this of book may be reproduced or transmitted in
Any form or by any means, graphic, electronic, or mechanical,
Including photocopying, recording, taping, or by any
Information storage or retrieval system, without the
Permission in writing from the publisher.

Purple Ink, Inc. Press

For Information address:
Purple Ink, Inc
P O Box 41232
Houston, TX 77241
www.purpleink.net
www.onediagage.com

ISBN:
978-1-939119-36-0

Printed in United States

Dedication

Hillary and Nehemiah,

I do not know what it takes to be my child, so I am praying for you.
This is for the teen you will be!
I love you! Very much!

Every teen I will meet!
Every teen I will minister to!
Every teen I will pray for!

Every teen who is in need of healing!
Every teen who is in need of prayer!
Every teen who is in need of rescue!
Every teen who is in need of recovery!
Every teen who is in need of restoration!
Every teen who is in need of dreams!

Every teen who is in need of LOVE!

The Notebook

God's Words

Hillary's Favorite

John 3:16 (NIV)

¹⁶For God so loved the world that He gave His one and only Son, that whoever believes in Him should not perish but have eternal life.

Minister Onedia's Favorites

1 Corinthians 13:13 (The Message)

¹³But for right now, until that completeness, we have three things to do to lead us toward that consummation: Trust steadily in God, Hope unswervingly, **Love extravagantly**. And the best of the three is love.

Ephesians 3:17b-19 (NIV)

¹⁷And I pray that you, being rooted and established in love, ¹⁸may have power, together with all the Lord's holy people, to grasp how wide and long and high and deep is the love of Christ, ¹⁹and to know this love that surpasses knowledge—that you may be filled to the measure of all the fullness of God.

The Notebook

For the Christian Teen

Dear God,

"Oh Lord, Our Lord how excellent is Thy name in the Earth!"

I know that You have ordered each step and ordained each moment. I cannot help sometimes but wonder about why me. In Your huge voice, You say why not you, Onedia. Lord, help me remain committed and compassionate to the generation which questions You and Your very existence. Help me Lord to remember that You are the Author and Finisher of all faiths. I am just a vessel. I am designed to do Your will.

Lord, thank You for forgiving me of my sins. I am so unworthy yet You allow me to serve in such magnificent ways. Lord, I am overwhelmed to see what You have done in my life, more than I could ever ask or think. I am so grateful that You chose me to do Your work. Thank You for the gifts You have bestowed me with, the ability and a platform to share those very gifts.

Lord, I know the only way to show You that I love You is to serve You by serving others and being obedient. I hope that while I struggle with consistent obedience, I will make You tremendously proud to serve You by serving others. Lord, I hope that my testimony will be a light to someone who wants to know You like I know You.

Lord, thank You for the calling on my life and all that it means to me, my family and others. I am working and praying daily to take care of it as You desire.

Lord, thank You for the young people that I will reach through this document. Thank You for my daughter, Hillary, who has chosen to take this journey and endeavor with me. I love her and I think the world of her. I thank You for making me her Mommy!

Lord, thank You again and in the awesome, powerful and remarkable name of Jesus I pray.

Amen.

The Notebook

For the Christian Teen

Dear Fellow Teen:

As the author's daughter, this book is very important to me because my mother and me came up with it. The first Notebook has gotten me through life so far, with the help of my extremely "rad" (radical) mother.

I love my mother very much! She is wise, loving, smart, a teacher, a writer, a mother, a mentor and more. The point is she is a fantabulous woman and is trying to raise me and my brother. Yes, she is doing it by herself but she is doing a great job.

I think it's a great book and will help you through some tough areas of your life. I hope that you will enjoy this journey with us.

Please do not hesitate to contact us.

Sincerely,

Hillary Nicole

Hillary Nicole
The daughter, Co-author

The Notebook

For the Christian Teen

Dear Christian Teen:

I must admit that the original Notebook was developed because of a troubled teen at a high school where I was a teacher. I realized that you needed a notebook as well.

When I spoke with Hillary about it—this new notebook, she overwhelmingly agreed. I am so excited about writing with her. So this notebook is for you. Please take full advantage of this opportunity. Please be honest with your answers for what will be revealed to you is for your personal growth. Use this to close the distance between you and God.

I am delighted that you are holding the spine of this book and that your eyes are passing over this page. This means that Christian growth and development is on the way.

I pray your closeness to God, a clearer understanding of Christ and His Lordship over our lives, and a will to follow Christ obediently.

Seek your depths. Share your whole self with Jesus. I pray your strength as you travel this journey.

I promise that you will have trouble in this life. I promise that you will have some drama in this life. I promise that you will have pain in this life. The place and the posture through this life will only come from Jesus. God promises that He will handle our burdens if we give them to Him. God promises that He will fight your battles if you would just be still (Exodus 14:14).

God is our fortress and our protection and our grace.

God is our definition of love. Others are supposed to embrace and enhance and reinforce that but even if they do not, your real definition is already set. Jesus loves you too.

The Notebook

The Notebook is for you, about you and by you, where God, Jesus and the Holy Spirit will walk you through your life.

Feel free to share with Hillary and me as you journey. You can follow me on twitter @onediangage, email onediagage@onediagage.com, facebook.com/onediagageministries, blogtalkradio.com/onediagage, and youtube.com/onediagage.

I can hardly wait!

In His Service!

Onedia N. Gage

Onedia N. Gage
www.onediagage.com

Dear Parents, Family, Church Leaders, and Advocates:

It is with an humble heart that I greet you today! I am praying for you in this journey. As a parent, minister, church leader, mentor, and child advocate, I am deeply invested in the lives of our children.

As a parent, I desire for God to meet my children's every need and I want to be a vessel. This Notebook is the answer to some of those needs and how I can be a vessel. I hope to help the voice and concerns through this book, these pages. Please use this to start a dialogue and to share your own story and your own journey. Communication usually makes relationships better. Use this to build on the relationship you have. Use this to add trust and confidence to your relationship.

As a minister and church leader, your child's life is harder and under attack based on your calling and role. Please continue to pray for them as they live with your role. They are on the clock with their own role and calling because of your role and legacy. Remember this is a huge responsibility for a young person who is still struggling to know his or her Creator. As a young person who is learning about God and themselves at the same time, we can be sure that they are overwhelmed. God still overwhelms me and I have been a Christian since I was six years old. I am still praying, listening, and remembering His will for my life.

As a mentor, I steer, lead, advise and counsel. You have to do that as well. This is a tough walk for both parties, however the journey is well worth all that goes into it. I have to be honest about me when I address our young people. Please do the same. We have an awesome opportunity to do what God called us to do and help to save their lives.

As a child advocate, I speak, advocate and journey with those who have no voice or a representative of their voice, so that they can have a chance at success as well.

The Notebook

Feel free to share with Hillary and me as you journey. You can follow us on twitter @onediangage, email onediagage@onediagage.com, facebook.com/onediagageministries, blogtalkradio.com/onediagage, and youtube.com/onediagage.

I can hardly wait!

In His Service!

Onedia N. Gage

Onedia N. Gage
www.onediagage.com

Instructions for Use

Write.
The Notebook for the Christian Teen was developed to provide you with an avenue of expression. It was adapted from the original version, The Notebook. As a classroom teacher, I had a student who was experiencing some difficulties with his life. **The Notebook** was created just for him. Upon reflection, Hillary and I decided that the Christian Teen needed one as well. You should respond to the questions honestly. Feel free to be transparent.

Share.
Share or don't share. Completely your choice. I find that when we write our feelings down, they are easier to share.

Save.
Save your own life. We need to get to a point of understanding ourselves so that we can function in a controlled environment. We want to respond when we have thought carefully and considered wisely the consequences of our actions. As a student and young person, almost an adult, you need to understand you are in training for the rest of your life. The problem I have is that we do not share those lessons in that manner. If I have the benefit of sharing what I see in store for you down the road, then I can share with you a best practice or method I know of that will help you get there efficiently. I am defining efficiently with the understanding that we are using the path with the least amount of trouble and the easiest way to reach the goal. This means that I am not going to always offer the short cut, yet I will offer the best method. Likewise, I want to teach how to make the correct decision in the future.

Time.
The time you spend in this notebook is for you. Use it selfishly and wisely!

The Notebook for the Christian Teen

The Notebook

For the Christian Teen

GOD'S HIGHER CALLING
By Onedia N. Gage

"Oh Lord, Our Lord, how excellent is thy name in all the Earth." Psalm 8:1

Lord, You have a higher calling for my life.
Lord, You have a divine plan for my being.
At Creation, Your will was to be done.

Lord, I want to be in Your will
Teach me Lord to walk in the steps of those of Jesus.

This higher calling of God's is hard to answer
Hard to comprehend
Harder to explain
Hardest to surrender

This Calling—Your will—is immeasurable yet dynamic.

This calling elevates me from the lustful desire
from the sinful nature
from the inexcusable activity
from the evil
from anything that inhibits my relationship with You, Christ

This calling demands my abundant giving
Compassionate spirit
Heartfelt love
At each moment of each day to ALL.

The Notebook

Lord, show me love and show me how to love
Lord, equip me to reach this calling
A calling where only You can receive the glory and the praise

Lord, heighten my spirituality to be the blessing You designed
Lord, You yearn for my obedience—make me yearn for my obedience

Lord, I Love You
I don't want to disappoint you
I don't want to miss nor misunderstand Your calling on my life

"A godly woman who can find?" Proverbs 31:10

God, I'm listening for the call.
    Your Higher Calling.

Reprinted from <u>The Blue Print: Poetry for the Soul</u>.

Table of Contents

Letters	9
Poem "God's Higher Calling"	23
The Questions	27
Appendix	155
Your Testimony	157
The Names of God	159
Prayer Directions	161
Prayer Request List/Journal	162
Favorite Scriptures	167
Goals	176
Mission	178
Vision	181
Values	185
Dreams	187
Resources	191
Acknowledgements	193
About the Inquisitors	195

The Notebook

26 | Minister Onedia and Hillary

For the Christian Teen

The Questions

For the Christian Teen

Who are you?
Who does God say you are? How does God define you?
How did you reach that definition?
How is this different from what God made you to be?
Is your definition of who you are defined by others? Who?
Why?
How much do you rely on God for your definition of yourself?

_____
_____
_____
_____
_____
_____
_____
_____
_____
_____
_____
_____
_____

Genesis 1:26-27 (NIV)

[26] Then God said, "Let us make mankind in our image, in our likeness, so that they may rule over the fish in the sea and the birds in the sky, over the livestock and all the wild animals,[a] and over all the creatures that move along the ground."

[27] So God created mankind in his own image,
  in the image of God he created them;
  male and female he created them.

The Notebook

Jeremiah 1:5 (NIV)

"Before I formed you in the womb I knew[a] you, before you were born I set you apart;
I appointed you as a prophet to the nations."

Does God approve of your definition?
Is your definition of yourself aligned with God's?
Why or why not?
Are you comfortable with who you are? Why or why not?
What can you do to abandon that definition if it does not align with God's definition?

_____
_____
_____
_____
_____
_____
_____
_____
_____
_____
_____
_____
_____
_____
_____
_____
_____

How are you defined by others? How do you know?
How did they reach that definition?
Are you comfortable with that definition? Why or why not?
Are you doing anything to change that definition?

_____
_____
_____
_____
_____
_____
_____
_____
_____
_____
_____
_____
_____
_____
_____
_____
_____

Psalm 139:14 (NIV)

[14] I praise you because I am fearfully and wonderfully made;
 your works are wonderful,
 I know that full well.

The Notebook

Matthew 6:28 (NIV)

²⁸ "And why do you worry about clothes? See how the flowers of the field grow. They do not labor or spin.

What would you change about yourself?
Why is that an important change?
Who supports that change?
What is the outcome of that change?
Will God be pleased with that change(s)?
Who are these changes really for: you, them or God?

_____
_____
_____
_____
_____
_____
_____
_____
_____
_____
_____
_____
_____
_____
_____

For the Christian Teen

What makes you happy?
What happens when you are happy?

_____
_____
_____
_____
_____
_____
_____
_____
_____
_____
_____
_____
_____
_____
_____
_____
_____
_____
_____

Ecclesiastes 3:12 (NIV)

¹² I know that there is nothing better for people than to be happy and to do good while they live.

The Notebook

John 15:11 (NIV)

¹¹ I have told you this so that my joy may be in you and that your joy may be complete.

Do you understand joy?
What is the difference between joy and happiness?
What is the source of joy?
Who do you know that has joy or is joyful?

_____
_____
_____
_____
_____
_____
_____
_____
_____
_____
_____
_____
_____
_____
_____
_____
_____

What disappoints God?
What do you do to disappoint God?
What disappoints you?
What happens when God is disappointed?
What happens when you are disappointed?

Psalm 90:7 (NIV)

⁷ We are consumed by your anger and terrified by your indignation.

_____
_____
_____
_____
_____
_____
_____
_____
_____
_____
_____
_____
_____
_____
_____
_____

The Notebook

The Names of God

What do you know about God (names, attributes, ways, etc.)?

Elohim: "Strong One"
El Shaddhai: "God almighty"
El Elyon: "The Most High God"
El Olam: "The Everlasting God"
Yahweh
Jehovah
Jehovah Jireh: "The Lord will provide"
Jehovah Nissi: "The Lord is my Banner"
Jehovah Shalom: "The Lord is Peach"
Jehovah Sabbaoth: "The Lord of Hosts"
Jehovah Maccaddeshcem: "The Lord your sanctifier"
Jehovah Ro'i: "The Lord my Shepherd"
Jehovah Tsidkenu: "The Lord our Righteousness"
Jehovah Shammah: "The Lord is there"
Jehovah Elohim: "The Lord, the God of Isreal"

_____
_____
_____
_____
_____
_____
_____
_____
_____
_____
_____
_____
_____
_____
_____
_____
_____
_____
_____
_____
_____

For the Christian Teen

What do you know about Jesus Christ (names, characteristics, behavior, etc.)?

_____
_____
_____
_____
_____
_____
_____
_____
_____
_____
_____
_____
_____
_____
_____
_____
_____

Hebrews 13:8 (NIV)

8 Jesus Christ is the same yesterday and today and forever.

Ephesians 6:24 (NIV)

24 Grace to all who love our Lord Jesus Christ with an undying love.

John 15:1 (NIV)

15 "I am the true vine, and my Father is the gardener.

The Notebook

Romans 8:26-27 (NIV)

²⁶ In the same way, the Spirit helps us in our weakness. We do not know what we ought to pray for, but the Spirit himself intercedes for us through wordless groans. ²⁷ And he who searches our hearts knows the mind of the Spirit, because the Spirit intercedes for God's people in accordance with the will of God.

Acts 13:52 (NIV)

⁵² And the disciples were filled with joy and with the Holy Spirit.

Luke 4:1 (NIV)

⁴ Jesus, full of the Holy Spirit, left the Jordan and was led by the Spirit into the wilderness,

What do you know about the Holy Spirit (definition, role, characteristics, etc.)?

_____
_____
_____
_____
_____
_____
_____
_____
_____
_____
_____
_____
_____
_____
_____
_____
_____
_____

For the Christian Teen

Is your Christian education important to you? Why or why not?
Do you take classes at church?
Does your youth ministry have church and activities designed just for you?

Psalm 119:68 (NIV)

[68] You are good, and what you do is good;
   teach me your decrees.

Luke 4:32 (NIV)

[32] They were amazed at his teaching, because his words had authority.

_____
_____
_____
_____
_____
_____
_____
_____
_____
_____
_____
_____
_____
_____
_____
_____

The Notebook

1 Corinthians 13:13 (MSG)

¹³ But for right now, until that completeness, we have three things to do to lead us toward that consummation: Trust steadily in God, hope unswervingly, love extravagantly. And the best of the three is love.

How does God define success?
How do you define success?
What can happen to align those definitions so that they are closer?

_____
_____
_____
_____
_____
_____
_____
_____
_____
_____
_____
_____
_____
_____
_____
_____
_____
_____

For the Christian Teen

How do you know that Christ loves you?
How much does Christ love you?
How much do you love Christ?

John 3:16 (NIV)

¹⁶ For God so loved the world that he gave his one and only Son, that whoever believes in him shall not perish but have eternal life.

_____
_____
_____
_____
_____
_____
_____
_____
_____
_____
_____
_____
_____
_____
_____
_____

The Notebook

Ephesians 2:8 (NIV)

⁸For it is by grace you have been saved, through faith—and this is not from yourselves, it is the gift of God

When did you first meet Jesus?
How did meeting Jesus change your life?

_____
_____
_____
_____
_____
_____
_____
_____
_____
_____
_____
_____
_____
_____
_____
_____
_____
_____

For the Christian Teen

Do you pray?
Do you know how to pray?
How did you learn to pray?

_____
_____
_____
_____
_____
_____
_____
_____
_____
_____
_____
_____
_____
_____

Matthew 6:5-15 (NIV)

⁹ "This, then, is how you should pray:

"'Our Father in heaven,
hallowed be your name,
¹⁰ your kingdom come,
your will be done,
   on earth as it is in heaven.
¹¹ Give us today our daily bread.
¹² And forgive us our debts,
   as we also have forgiven our debtors.
¹³ And lead us not into temptation,
   but deliver us from the evil one.

The Notebook

John 17:9 (NIV)

⁹ I pray for them. I am not praying for the world, but for those you have given me, for they are yours.

Why do you pray?
Who do you pray for? Make a list.
Who knows that you pray? How do they know?
Do others ask you to pray for them?

_____
_____
_____
_____
_____
_____
_____
_____
_____
_____
_____
_____
_____
_____
_____
_____
_____
_____
_____

For the Christian Teen

Who do you know that prays?
Do you listen to them pray?
Do you ask that prayer warrior to pray for you?
Do you ask that prayer warrior to pray with you?

Luke 22:31 (NIV)

[31] "Simon, Simon, Satan has asked to sift all of you as wheat.

_____
_____
_____
_____
_____
_____
_____
_____
_____
_____
_____
_____
_____
_____
_____
_____
_____

The Notebook

John 16:24 (NIV)

²⁴ Until now you have not asked for anything in my name. Ask and you will receive, and your joy will be complete.

Matthew 26:36 (NIV)

³⁶ Then Jesus went with his disciples to a place called Gethsemane, and he said to them, "Sit here while I go over there and pray."

What are you praying for?
What are you asking God for?
Do you pray during tests?

_____
_____
_____
_____
_____
_____
_____
_____
_____
_____
_____
_____
_____
_____
_____
_____
_____

For the Christian Teen

When have you seen God answer your prayers?
What prayer(s) did God answer?
What did God say?

_____
_____
_____
_____
_____
_____
_____
_____
_____
_____
_____
_____
_____
_____
_____

1 Kings 3:10-14 (NIV)

[10] The Lord was pleased that Solomon had asked for this. [11] So God said to him, "Since you have asked for this and not for long life or wealth for yourself, nor have asked for the death of your enemies but for discernment in administering justice, [12] I will do what you have asked. I will give you a wise and discerning heart, so that there will never have been anyone like you, nor will there ever be.
[13] Moreover, I will give you what you have not asked for—both wealth and honor—so that in your lifetime you will have no equal among kings. [14] And if you walk in obedience to me and keep my decrees and commands as David your father did, I will give you a long life."

The Notebook

Matthew 26:34-35 (NIV)

[34] "Truly I tell you," Jesus answered, "this very night, before the rooster crows, you will disown me three times."

[35] But Peter declared, "Even if I have to die with you, I will never disown you." And all the other disciples said the same.

Do your friends know that you are a Christian? How do they know you are a Christian?

_____
_____
_____
_____
_____
_____
_____
_____
_____
_____
_____
_____
_____
_____
_____
_____
_____
_____

For the Christian Teen

Are your friends Christian?
How do you know?

Luke 9:23 (NIV)

[23] Then he said to them all: "Whoever wants to be my disciple must deny themselves and take up their cross daily and follow me.

The Notebook

Acts 2:42-44 (NIV)

⁴² They devoted themselves to the apostles' teaching and to fellowship, to the breaking of bread and to prayer. ⁴³ Everyone was filled with awe at the many wonders and signs performed by the apostles. ⁴⁴ All the believers were together and had everything in common.

Who have you invited to visit church?
How often do you invite someone to visit church?

_____
_____
_____
_____
_____
_____
_____
_____
_____
_____
_____
_____
_____
_____
_____
_____
_____
_____

What do you want God to call you to do?
What are your spiritual gifts?

_____
_____
_____
_____
_____
_____
_____
_____
_____
_____
_____
_____
_____
_____
_____
_____

For the Christian Teen

1 Corinthians 12:7-11 (NIV)

[7] Now to each one the manifestation of the Spirit is given for the common good. [8] To one there is given through the Spirit a message of wisdom, to another a message of knowledge by means of the same Spirit, [9] to another faith by the same Spirit, to another gifts of healing by that one Spirit, [10] to another miraculous powers, to another prophecy, to another distinguishing between spirits, to another speaking in different kinds of tongues,[a] and to still another the interpretation of tongues.[b] [11] All these are the work of one and the same Spirit, and he distributes them to each one, just as he determines.

The Notebook

Matthew 10:4 (NIV)

⁴ Simon the Zealot and Judas Iscariot, who betrayed him.

Is there anything that would cause you to walk away from God?

_____
_____
_____
_____
_____
_____
_____
_____
_____
_____
_____
_____
_____
_____
_____
_____
_____
_____
_____

For the Christian Teen

How do you explain why God is real to you?
Do you feel comfortable explaining this about God?

_____
_____
_____
_____
_____
_____
_____
_____
_____
_____
_____
_____
_____
_____
_____
_____
_____
_____

Exodus 6:10-11 (NIV)

[10] Then the LORD said to Moses, [11] "Go, tell Pharaoh king of Egypt to let the Israelites go out of his country."

The Notebook

Matthew 6:27 (NIV)

²⁷ Can any one of you by worrying add a single hour to your life?

What do you worry about?
What does God say about worry?

_____
_____
_____
_____
_____
_____
_____
_____
_____
_____
_____
_____
_____
_____
_____
_____
_____
_____
_____
_____

For the Christian Teen

What burdens you?
What does Jesus say about your burdens?
Why is it so difficult to give Jesus your burdens?

Matthew 11:28-30 (NIV)

²⁸ "Come to me, all you who are weary and burdened, and I will give you rest. ²⁹ Take my yoke upon you and learn from me, for I am gentle and humble in heart, and you will find rest for your souls. ³⁰ For my yoke is easy and my burden is light."

Minister Onedia and Hillary

The Notebook

Genesis 4:6 (NIV)

⁶ Then the LORD said to Cain, "Why are you angry? Why is your face downcast?

Psalm 55:5 (NIV)

⁵ Fear and trembling have beset me;
 horror has overwhelmed me.

Does God respond when we are moody and temperamental? What determines your mood each day?

_____
_____
_____
_____
_____
_____
_____
_____
_____
_____
_____
_____
_____
_____
_____
_____
_____

For the Christian Teen

Who/What makes you angry?
What determines how long you stay angry?
What do you do to resolve that anger?
What does God want us to do when we are angry?
What did Jesus do when He was angry?

Ecclesiastes 7:9 (NIV)

⁹ Do not be quickly provoked in your spirit,
    for anger resides in the lap of fools.

Ephesians 4:26-27 (NIV)

²⁶ "In your anger do not sin": Do not let the sun go down while you are still angry, ²⁷ and do not give the devil a foothold.

The Notebook

Genesis 4:8-9 (NIV)

⁸ Now Cain said to his brother Abel, "Let's go out to the field."[a] While they were in the field, Cain attacked his brother Abel and killed him.

⁹ Then the LORD said to Cain, "Where is your brother Abel?"

"I don't know," he replied. "Am I my brother's keeper?"

Do you know the story of Cain and Abel?
How do you feel about your family?
Why?
Is there a particular event that caused these feelings?

_____
_____
_____
_____
_____
_____
_____
_____
_____
_____
_____
_____
_____
_____
_____
_____

For the Christian Teen

Do you know the story of Joseph and his brothers?
How does your family feel about you? Why?
Is there a particular event that caused these feelings?

_____
_____
_____
_____
_____
_____
_____
_____
_____
_____
_____
_____
_____

Genesis 37:31-34 (NIV)

[31] Then they got Joseph's robe, slaughtered a goat and dipped the robe in the blood. [32] They took the ornate robe back to their father and said, "We found this. Examine it to see whether it is your son's robe."

[33] He recognized it and said, "It is my son's robe! Some ferocious animal has devoured him. Joseph has surely been torn to pieces."

[34] Then Jacob tore his clothes, put on sackcloth and mourned for his son many days.

The Notebook

Genesis 16:15-16 (NIV)

¹⁵ So Hagar bore Abram a son, and Abram gave the name Ishmael to the son she had borne. ¹⁶ Abram was eighty-six years old when Hagar bore him Ishmael.

Do you know the story of Abraham, Sarah, Haggar, Issac and Ishmael?
How is your family defined? Feel free to draw a picture, if desired.

_____
_____
_____
_____
_____
_____
_____
_____
_____
_____
_____
_____
_____
_____
_____
_____
_____

Do you know the story of Noah?
How do you feel about your family structure/dynamics?

_____
_____
_____
_____
_____
_____
_____
_____
_____
_____
_____
_____
_____
_____
_____

Genesis 6:18-22 (NIV)

[18] But I will establish my covenant with you, and you will enter the ark—you and your sons and your wife and your sons' wives with you. [19] You are to bring into the ark two of all living creatures, male and female, to keep them alive with you. [20] Two of every kind of bird, of every kind of animal and of every kind of creature that moves along the ground will come to you to be kept alive. [21] You are to take every kind of food that is to be eaten and store it away as food for you and for them."

[22] Noah did everything just as God commanded him.

The Notebook

Matthew 1:18 (NIV)

¹⁸ This is how the birth of Jesus the Messiah came about: His mother Mary was pledged to be married to Joseph, but before they came together, she was found to be pregnant through the Holy Spirit.

Do you know the story of Joseph, Mary, and Jesus?
If you could pick your family, would you pick the one you have? Why?
If not, who would you pick as a family? Why?

_____
_____
_____
_____
_____
_____
_____
_____
_____
_____
_____
_____
_____
_____
_____
_____
_____
_____

For the Christian Teen

Do you know the story of David?
What are important family values for you?
How did you learn these values?
Are these currently functioning in your home?

_____
_____
_____
_____
_____
_____
_____
_____
_____
_____
_____
_____
_____
_____
_____
_____
_____

1 Samuel 16:5, 7, 12 (NIV)

⁵ Samuel replied, "Yes, in peace; I have come to sacrifice to the LORD. Consecrate yourselves and come to the sacrifice with me." Then he consecrated Jesse and his sons and invited them to the sacrifice.
⁷ But the LORD said to Samuel, "Do not consider his appearance or his height, for I have rejected him. The LORD does not look at the things people look at. People look at the outward appearance, but the LORD looks at the heart."

¹² So he sent for him and had him brought in. He was glowing with health and had a fine appearance and handsome features.

Then the LORD said, "Rise and anoint him; this is the one."

The Notebook

Job 1:1-3 (NIV)

¹ In the land of Uz there lived a man whose name was Job. This man was blameless and upright; he feared God and shunned evil. ² He had seven sons and three daughters, ³ and he owned seven thousand sheep, three thousand camels, five hundred yoke of oxen and five hundred donkeys, and had a large number of servants. He was the greatest man among all the people of the East.

Do you know the story of Job and Noah?
What should a family do and be?
What makes someone family?

_____
_____
_____
_____
_____
_____
_____
_____
_____
_____
_____
_____
_____
_____
_____
_____
_____

For the Christian Teen

Do you know the story of Ruth to David to Jesus?
What is your family legacy?
Consider family education, businesses owned,
homeownership, and overall activities.

_____
_____
_____
_____
_____
_____
_____
_____
_____
_____
_____
_____
_____

Matthew 1:1-16 (NIV)

Ruth 1:16 (NIV)

[8] Then Naomi said to her two daughters-in-law, "Go back, each of you, to your mother's home. May the LORD show you kindness, as you have shown kindness to your dead husbands and to me. [9] May the LORD grant that each of you will find rest in the home of another husband." [16] But Ruth replied, "Don't urge me to leave you or to turn back from you. Where you go I will go, and where you stay I will stay. Your people will be my people and your God my God.

The Notebook

Ruth 1:16-18 (NIV)

¹⁶ But Ruth replied, "Don't urge me to leave you or to turn back from you. Where you go I will go, and where you stay I will stay. Your people will be my people and your God my God. ¹⁷ Where you die I will die, and there I will be buried. May the LORD deal with me, be it ever so severely, if even death separates you and me." ¹⁸ When Naomi realized that Ruth was determined to go with her, she stopped urging her.

Who is your favorite family member?
Why? What makes someone family?
How much time do you spend with him/her?
What kind of activities do you do when you are together?

_____
_____
_____
_____
_____
_____
_____
_____
_____
_____
_____
_____
_____
_____
_____

For the Christian Teen

Do you know the verses Titus 2:1-8?
Do you have a person that does this for you?
Have you learned well enough to help your future children with their homework?

_____
_____
_____
_____
_____
_____
_____
_____
_____
_____
_____
_____
_____
_____
_____

Titus 2:1-3 (NIV)

¹You, however, must teach what is appropriate to sound doctrine. ²Teach the older men to be temperate, worthy of respect, self-controlled, and sound in faith, in love and in endurance.

³Likewise, teach the older women to be reverent in the way they live, not to be slanderers or addicted to much wine, but to teach what is good.

The Notebook

Proverbs 14:20 (NIV)

²⁰ The poor are shunned even by their neighbors,
  but the rich have many friends.

Matthew 6:19-20 (NIV)

¹⁹ "Do not store up for yourselves treasures on earth, where moths and vermin destroy, and where thieves break in and steal. ²⁰ But store up for yourselves treasures in heaven, where moths and vermin do not destroy, and where thieves do not break in and steal. ²¹ For where your treasure is, there your heart will be also.

Are rich and poor important to you? How do you define rich and poor? Are you rich or poor?
How does God address riches?
Do you let rich/poor define who you are?
Are you willing to adopt God's definition of riches and abandon your own?

_____
_____
_____
_____
_____
_____
_____
_____
_____
_____
_____
_____
_____

For the Christian Teen

What does God say about money?

_____
_____
_____
_____
_____
_____
_____
_____
_____
_____
_____
_____
_____
_____
_____
_____
_____

1 Timothy 3:3 (NIV)

³ not given to drunkenness, not violent but gentle, not quarrelsome, not a lover of money.

Proverbs 13:11 (NIV)

¹¹ Dishonest money dwindles away,
    but whoever gathers money little by little makes it grow.

The Notebook

Leviticus 25:35-37 (NIV)

35 "'If any of your fellow Israelites become poor and are unable to support themselves among you, help them as you would a foreigner and stranger, so they can continue to live among you. 36 Do not take interest or any profit from them, but fear your God, so that they may continue to live among you. 37 You must not lend them money at interest or sell them food at a profit.

Should you feel guilty about God blessing you with money if others close to you do not have enough?

_____
_____
_____
_____
_____
_____
_____
_____
_____
_____
_____
_____
_____
_____
_____
_____
_____
_____

For the Christian Teen

What would you do with $100,000?
Would you give 10% to the church?
Who would you tell first?
Who do you know or know of with this amount of money?

_____
_____
_____
_____
_____
_____
_____
_____
_____
_____
_____
_____
_____
_____

Malachi 3:10 (NIV)

¹⁰ Bring the whole tithe into the storehouse, that there may be food in my house. Test me in this," says the LORD Almighty, "and see if I will not throw open the floodgates of heaven and pour out so much blessing that there will not be room enough to store it.

The Notebook

1 Timothy 6:10 (NIV)

¹⁰ For the love of money is a root of all kinds of evil. Some people, eager for money, have wandered from the faith and pierced themselves with many griefs.

What would you do with $1 million?
Would you give 10% to the church?
Who would you tell first?
Who do you know or know of with this amount of money?

_____
_____
_____
_____
_____
_____
_____
_____
_____
_____
_____
_____
_____
_____
_____
_____
_____

For the Christian Teen

What would you do with $10 million?
Would you give 10% to the church?
Who would you tell first?
Who do you know or know of with that amount of money?

_____
_____
_____
_____
_____
_____
_____
_____
_____
_____
_____
_____
_____
_____
_____

Proverbs 17:16 (NIV)

[16] Why should fools have money in hand to buy wisdom,
  when they are not able to understand it?

Ecclesiastes 7:12 (NIV)

[12] Wisdom is a shelter
  as money is a shelter,
but the advantage of knowledge is this:
  Wisdom preserves those who have it.

The Notebook

1 Samuel 26:22-24 (NIV)

²²"Here is the king's spear," David answered. "Let one of your young men come over and get it. ²³ The LORD rewards everyone for their righteousness and faithfulness. The LORD delivered you into my hands today, but I would not lay a hand on the LORD's anointed. ²⁴ As surely as I valued your life today, so may the LORD value my life and deliver me from all trouble."

Who does God want us to value?
Who do you value?
Why?

_____
_____
_____
_____
_____
_____
_____
_____
_____
_____
_____
_____
_____
_____
_____
_____

What does God want us to value?
What do you value?
Why?

_____
_____
_____
_____
_____
_____
_____
_____
_____
_____
_____
_____
_____
_____
_____
_____

Isaiah 52:3 (NIV)

³ For this is what the LORD says:

"You were sold for nothing,
 and without money you will be redeemed."

The Notebook

Proverbs 18:24 (NIV)

²⁴ One who has unreliable friends soon comes to ruin,
   but there is a friend who sticks closer than a brother.

Who is your best friend? Why?
What does God say about friends?

_____
_____
_____
_____
_____
_____
_____
_____
_____
_____
_____
_____
_____
_____
_____
_____
_____
_____
_____
_____

For the Christian Teen

Does your friend know Christ?
If not, do you plan to share Jesus with your best friend?
Do you understand why Jesus said that He is our friend?

_____
_____
_____
_____
_____
_____
_____
_____
_____
_____
_____
_____
_____
_____

Matthew 28:19-20 (NIV)

[19] Therefore go and make disciples of all nations, baptizing them in the name of the Father and of the Son and of the Holy Spirit, [20] and teaching them to obey everything I have commanded you. And surely I am with you always, to the very end of the age."

The Notebook

John 3:16 (NIV)

¹⁶ For God so loved the world that he gave his one and only Son, that whoever believes in him shall not perish but have eternal life.

What has been the best thing that God has ever done to/for you?
Why?

_____
_____
_____
_____
_____
_____
_____
_____
_____
_____
_____
_____
_____
_____
_____
_____
_____
_____

What has been the second best thing that God has ever done to/for you?
Why?

_____
_____
_____
_____
_____
_____
_____
_____
_____
_____
_____
_____
_____
_____
_____
_____
_____

For the Christian Teen

Matthew 6:14-15 (NIV)

^{14} For if you forgive other people when they sin against you, your heavenly Father will also forgive you. ^{15} But if you do not forgive others their sins, your Father will not forgive your sins.

The Notebook

1 Samuel 3:9-11 (NIV)

⁹ So Eli told Samuel, "Go and lie down, and if he calls you, say, 'Speak, LORD, for your servant is listening.'" So Samuel went and lay down in his place.

¹⁰ The LORD came and stood there, calling as at the other times, "Samuel! Samuel!"

Then Samuel said, "Speak, for your servant is listening."

¹¹ And the LORD said to Samuel: "See, I am about to do something in Israel that will make the ears of everyone who hears about it tingle.

What age do you first remember listening to God?
What age do you first remember knowing God and Jesus?
What did you first learn about Christ?

_____
_____
_____
_____
_____
_____
_____
_____
_____
_____
_____
_____
_____
_____
_____
_____

For the Christian Teen

What is the worst aspect of your childhood? Why?
Did you share this with God?
What did God say?

_____
_____
_____
_____
_____
_____
_____
_____
_____
_____
_____
_____
_____
_____

Mark 7:25-26, 29-30 (NIV)

[25] In fact, as soon as she heard about him, a woman whose little daughter was possessed by an impure spirit came and fell at his feet. [26] The woman was a Greek, born in Syrian Phoenicia. She begged Jesus to drive the demon out of her daughter.

[29] Then he told her, "For such a reply, you may go; the demon has left your daughter."

[30] She went home and found her child lying on the bed, and the demon gone.

The Notebook

Psalm 98:2-3 (NIV)

² The LORD has made his salvation known and revealed his righteousness to the nations.
³ He has remembered his love and his faithfulness to Israel; all the ends of the earth have seen the salvation of our God.

What is your favorite part of your knowledge of God? Why?

_____
_____
_____
_____
_____
_____
_____
_____
_____
_____
_____
_____
_____
_____
_____
_____
_____
_____
_____

For the Christian Teen

What is the worst thing you have ever experienced? Did you tell Jesus about it? What did Jesus say? Who did you share that with? What did they say?

_____
_____
_____
_____
_____
_____
_____
_____
_____
_____
_____
_____
_____
_____
_____
_____

Job 2:6-7 (NIV)

⁶ The LORD said to Satan, "Very well, then, he is in your hands; but you must spare his life."

⁷ So Satan went out from the presence of the LORD and afflicted Job with painful sores from the soles of his feet to the crown of his head.

The Notebook

Matthew 14:10-12 (NIV)

¹⁰ and had John beheaded in the prison. ¹¹ His head was brought in on a platter and given to the girl, who carried it to her mother. ¹² John's disciples came and took his body and buried it. Then they went and told Jesus.

How do you share that Jesus died for your sins?
Have you ever experienced the death of someone close to you in age?
Have you ever experienced the death of someone in your family?
Who? How did it make you feel?

_____
_____
_____
_____
_____
_____
_____
_____
_____
_____
_____
_____
_____
_____

For the Christian Teen

How long did it take you to recover from the death of that person(s)?
How long did it take for you to stop being angry?
Did you blame or hate God for that death? Why?

_____
_____
_____
_____
_____
_____
_____
_____
_____
_____
_____
_____
_____
_____

John 11:21-22, 35 (NIV)

[21] "Lord," Martha said to Jesus, "if you had been here, my brother would not have died. [22] But I know that even now God will give you whatever you ask."

[35] Jesus wept.

The Notebook

Matthew 27:5 (NIV)

⁵ So Judas threw the money into the temple and left. Then he went away and hanged himself.

Is suicide a sin?
Is it forgivable by God?
Is it necessary? Are your issues so much bigger than God that you consider such a permanent option?

_____
_____
_____
_____
_____
_____
_____
_____
_____
_____
_____
_____
_____
_____
_____
_____
_____
_____

What made those thoughts of suicide cross your mind?
What made you fail to try?
What made the attempt fail? Why?

_____
_____
_____
_____
_____
_____
_____
_____
_____
_____
_____
_____
_____
_____
_____

Luke 22:47-48 (NIV)

⁴⁷ While he was still speaking a crowd came up, and the man who was called Judas, one of the Twelve, was leading them. He approached Jesus to kiss him, ⁴⁸ but Jesus asked him, "Judas, are you betraying the Son of Man with a kiss?"

The Notebook

Acts 1:18 (NIV)

¹⁸ (With the payment he received for his wickedness, Judas bought a field; there he fell headlong, his body burst open and all his intestines spilled out.

Have your friends considered suicide?
What did you say when they told you?
Do you have someone you can ask for help when this happens for them and for you?

_____
_____
_____
_____
_____
_____
_____
_____
_____
_____
_____
_____
_____
_____
_____
_____
_____

For the Christian Teen

Has your heart ever been broken? By whom?
Did you ask Jesus to heal you from that hurt?
Has the hurt subsided? Are you healed?
How long did it take to heal?

_____
_____
_____
_____
_____
_____
_____
_____
_____
_____
_____
_____
_____
_____
_____
_____

Psalm 73:21-22 (NIV)

[21] When my heart was grieved and my spirit embittered,
[22] I was senseless and ignorant; I was a brute beast before you.

The Notebook

1 John 4:19 (NIV)

¹⁹ We love because he first loved us.

John 15:12 (NIV)

¹² My command is this: Love each other as I have loved you.

Have you ever been in love?
How did you feel when you were in love?
How long did it last?
Do you look forward to it happening again?
What does Paul say about this type of love?

_____
_____
_____
_____
_____
_____
_____
_____
_____
_____
_____
_____
_____
_____
_____
_____
_____

For the Christian Teen

How does God define love?
How do you define love?

_____
_____
_____
_____
_____
_____
_____
_____
_____
_____
_____
_____
_____
_____
_____

1 John 4:10 (NIV)

¹⁰ This is love: not that we loved God, but that he loved us and sent his Son as an atoning sacrifice for our sins.

1 John 2:15 (NIV)

¹⁵ Do not love the world or anything in the world. If anyone loves the world, love for the Father[a] is not in them.

Minister Onedia and Hillary | 91

The Notebook

Proverbs 8:17 (NIV)

¹⁷ I love those who love me, and those who seek me find me.

John 16:27 (NIV)

¹⁷ At this, some of his disciples said to one another, "What does he mean by saying, 'In a little while you will see me no more, and then after a little while you will see me,' and 'Because I am going to the Father'?"

Who loves you?
Whom do you love?
Is love important to you?

_____
_____
_____
_____
_____
_____
_____
_____
_____
_____
_____
_____
_____
_____
_____
_____
_____

How does Jesus know that you love Him?
Obedience? Words? Actions? Service to others? Sacrifice?

_____
_____
_____
_____
_____
_____
_____
_____
_____
_____
_____
_____
_____
_____
_____
_____

2 John 1:6 (NIV)

⁶ And this is love: that we walk in obedience to his commands. As you have heard from the beginning, his command is that you walk in love.

John 14:15 (NIV)

¹⁵ "If you love me, keep my commands.

The Notebook

Philippians 2:1-8 (NIV)

⁵ In your relationships with one another, have the same mindset as Christ Jesus:

⁶ Who, being in very nature[a] God,
   did not consider equality with God something to be used to his own advantage;
⁷ rather, he made himself nothing
   by taking the very nature[b] of a servant,
   being made in human likeness.

What is important to God for you?
What is important to you (either material or intangible)?
How far apart is that definition from God's?
What can't you live without?
Why?

_____
_____
_____
_____
_____
_____
_____
_____
_____
_____
_____
_____
_____
_____
_____
_____

For the Christian Teen

Why did God make parents?
What does God say we are to do as parents?
How could you honor your parents better?
When and why is honoring them hard for you?
If you could pick different parents, who would they be or what would they be like?

1 Samuel 1:20 (NIV)

[20] So in the course of time Hannah became pregnant and gave birth to a son. She named him Samuel,[a] saying, "Because I asked the LORD for him.

The Notebook

1 Samuel 1:22-23, 28 (NIV)

²² Hannah did not go. She said to her husband, "After the boy is weaned, I will take him and present him before the LORD, and he will live there always."[a]

²³ "Do what seems best to you," her husband Elkanah told her. "Stay here until you have weaned him; only may the LORD make good his[b] word." So the woman stayed at home and nursed her son until she had weaned him.

²⁸ So now I give him to the LORD. For his whole life he will be given over to the LORD." And he worshiped the LORD there.

Who do you define as a great parent?
What are you going to do as a parent when you are one?
What are you NOT going to do as a parent?

_____
_____
_____
_____
_____
_____
_____
_____
_____
_____
_____
_____
_____
_____
_____
_____
_____

For the Christian Teen

Do you have a role model?
Do you admire their relationship with Christ?
Who is it?
How did you select that person as your role model?

_____
_____
_____
_____
_____
_____
_____
_____
_____
_____
_____
_____
_____
_____
_____

Luke 1:42-44 (NIV)

[42] In a loud voice she exclaimed: "Blessed are you among women, and blessed is the child you will bear! [43] But why am I so favored, that the mother of my Lord should come to me? [44] As soon as the sound of your greeting reached my ears, the baby in my womb leaped for joy.

The Notebook

Titus 2:1-4 (NIV)

You, however, must teach what is appropriate to sound doctrine. ²Teach the older men to be temperate, worthy of respect, self-controlled, and sound in faith, in love and in endurance.

³Likewise, teach the older women to be reverent in the way they live, not to be slanderers or addicted to much wine, but to teach what is good. ⁴Then they can urge the younger women to love their husbands and children,

Who is your favorite person at church?
Who do you admire at church?
Why?

_____
_____
_____
_____
_____
_____
_____
_____
_____
_____
_____
_____
_____
_____
_____
_____

For the Christian Teen

What is your favorite scripture(s)?

2 Timothy 2:15 (NIV)

[15] Do your best to present yourself to God as one approved, a worker who does not need to be ashamed and who correctly handles the word of truth.

Matthew 22-29 (NIV)

[29] Jesus replied, "You are in error because you do not know the Scriptures or the power of God.

The Notebook

Psalm 150:1 (NIV)

[1] Praise the LORD.[a]

Praise God in his sanctuary;
   praise him in his mighty heavens.

Psalm 66:8 (NIV)

[8] Praise our God, all peoples,
   let the sound of his praise be heard;

What is your favorite part of church? Why?

_____
_____
_____
_____
_____
_____
_____
_____
_____
_____
_____
_____
_____
_____
_____
_____
_____
_____

For the Christian Teen

Who is your favorite Biblical character?
What would you say if you could meet them? Why?

_____
_____
_____
_____
_____
_____
_____
_____
_____
_____
_____
_____
_____
_____
_____

Matthew 14:29 (NIV)

²⁹ "Come," he said.

Then Peter got down out of the boat, walked on the water and came toward Jesus.

Jesus

David

Hannah

Peter

Paul

The Notebook

Exodus 34:17 (NIV)

¹⁷ "Do not make any idols.

Who is your favorite Christian actor/actress/TV personality/musician?
Why?
If you met them, what would you say?
How would you want to spend that time?

_____
_____
_____
_____
_____
_____
_____
_____
_____
_____
_____
_____
_____
_____
_____
_____

For the Christian Teen

What will you say to God when you get to heaven?
What questions do you have of God?

_____
_____
_____
_____
_____
_____
_____
_____
_____
_____
_____
_____
_____
_____
_____
_____

Matthew 5:3 (NIV)

3 "Blessed are the poor in spirit,
  for theirs is the kingdom of heaven.

Mark 12:18 (NIV)

18 Then the Sadducees, who say there is no resurrection, came to him with a question.

Luke 20:40 (NIV)

40 And no one dared to ask him any more questions.

The Notebook

Exodus 3:5 (NIV)

⁵ "Do not come any closer," God said. "Take off your sandals, for the place where you are standing is holy ground."

Have you ever been to a Christian camp?
Would you like to go?
What would/did you take away from that experience?
What would you tell another student to encourage them to be a part of that camp next time?

_____
_____
_____
_____
_____
_____
_____
_____
_____
_____
_____
_____
_____
_____
_____
_____

For the Christian Teen

How do you feel about your current life?
What would God say about your current life?
Why?
What can you do to make it better?

_____
_____
_____
_____
_____
_____
_____
_____
_____
_____
_____
_____
_____
_____
_____

Matthew 6:32-34 (NIV)

³² For the pagans run after all these things, and your heavenly Father knows that you need them. ³³ But seek first his kingdom and his righteousness, and all these things will be given to you as well. ³⁴ Therefore do not worry about tomorrow, for tomorrow will worry about itself. Each day has enough trouble of its own.

The Notebook

Jeremiah 29:11 (NIV)

¹¹ For I know the plans I have for you," declares the LORD, "plans to prosper you and not to harm you, plans to give you hope and a future.

When you consider the plans you have for yourself, how do you think they align with God's plans for you?

_____
_____
_____
_____
_____
_____
_____
_____
_____
_____
_____
_____
_____
_____
_____
_____
_____
_____
_____
_____
_____

For the Christian Teen

What is your definition of fun?
What is the most fun you have ever had?
Could you have fun with Jesus in the room?
Why or why not?

Proverbs 5:23 (NIV)

²³ For lack of discipline they will die,
  led astray by their own great folly.

_____
_____
_____
_____
_____
_____
_____
_____
_____
_____
_____
_____
_____
_____
_____
_____

The Notebook

Matthew 22:34-35 (NIV)

³⁴ Hearing that Jesus had silenced the Sadducees, the Pharisees got together. ³⁵ One of them, an expert in the law, tested him with this question:

Define a gang or clique.
Would you consider joining a gang?
Do you know anyone in a gang?
What would you do if the gang tried to get you to join?
Do you know that you can realize God's forgiveness?

_____
_____
_____
_____
_____
_____
_____
_____
_____
_____
_____
_____
_____
_____
_____
_____
_____

What are your favorite Christian songs?

_____
_____
_____
_____
_____
_____
_____
_____
_____
_____
_____
_____
_____
_____
_____
_____
_____
_____

For the Christian Teen

1 Chronicles 15:28 (NIV)

[28] So all Israel brought up the ark of the covenant of the LORD with shouts, with the sounding of rams' horns and trumpets, and of cymbals, and the playing of lyres and harps.

The Notebook

Genesis 7:5 (NIV)

⁵ And Noah did all that the LORD commanded him.

What are your favorite Christian movies?

_____
_____
_____
_____
_____
_____
_____
_____
_____
_____
_____
_____
_____
_____
_____
_____
_____
_____
_____
_____
_____
_____

What is your favorite Christian celebration?
Why?
What do you do on those days?

_____
_____
_____
_____
_____
_____
_____
_____
_____
_____
_____
_____
_____
_____
_____
_____
_____

Matthew 26:19 (NIV)

¹⁹ So the disciples did as Jesus had directed them and prepared the Passover.

Matthew 1:18 (NIV)

¹⁸ This is how the birth of Jesus the Messiah came about[a]: His mother Mary was pledged to be married to Joseph, but before they came together, she was found to be pregnant through the Holy Spirit.

John 20:17 (NIV)

¹⁷ Jesus said, "Do not hold on to me, for I have not yet ascended to the Father. Go instead to my brothers and tell them, 'I am ascending to my Father and your Father, to my God and your God.'"

The Notebook

1 Corinthians 12:4-7 (NIV)

⁴ There are different kinds of gifts, but the same Spirit distributes them. ⁵ There are different kinds of service, but the same Lord. ⁶ There are different kinds of working, but in all of them and in everyone it is the same God at work.

⁷ Now to each one the manifestation of the Spirit is given for the common good.

Do you write as an escape (like poetry, songs, raps or essays)? What does this writing do to help you navigate life's journey? How could you use your writing gifts to help God bring others to Christ?

_____
_____
_____
_____
_____
_____
_____
_____
_____
_____
_____
_____
_____
_____
_____
_____
_____

For the Christian Teen

Write God a love letter.

Deuteronomy 6:5 (NIV)

[5] Love the LORD your God with all your heart and with all your soul and with all your strength.

Matthew 22:37 (NIV)

[37] Jesus replied: "'Love the Lord your God with all your heart and with all your soul and with all your mind.

The Notebook

Joel 1:3 (NIV)

³ Tell it to your children,
  and let your children
tell it to their children,
  and their children to
the next generation.

What part of your childhood will you share with your child?
Why?
Why did God allow that to happen?

_____
_____
_____
_____
_____
_____
_____
_____
_____
_____
_____
_____
_____
_____
_____
_____
_____
_____

For the Christian Teen

What does God say about respect?
Define respect.
Who do you respect?
Who respects you? Do you demand respect?
Why?

_____
_____
_____
_____
_____
_____
_____
_____
_____
_____
_____
_____
_____

Ephesians 6:1-4 (NIV)

6 Children, obey your parents in the Lord, for this is right. ² "Honor your father and mother"— which is the first commandment with a promise— ³ "so that it may go well with you and that you may enjoy long life on the earth."

The Notebook

Proverbs 13:13 (NIV)

[13] Whoever scorns instruction will pay for it,
   but whoever respects a command is rewarded.

1 Timothy 3:11 (NIV)

[11] In the same way, the women[a] are to be worthy of respect, not malicious talkers but temperate and trustworthy in everything.

What does it take to earn your respect?
How does God know that you respect Him?
List persons whom you respect.

_____
_____
_____
_____
_____
_____
_____
_____
_____
_____
_____
_____
_____
_____
_____
_____
_____
_____
_____
_____

For the Christian Teen

Define forgiveness from God's definition.
Who have you had to forgive?
Why?
Was it hard?
God forgives everything. Why is it hard for you?
Jesus told us to forgive limitlessly. Why do we keep count?
Why do we hold grudges?

_____
_____
_____
_____
_____
_____
_____
_____
_____
_____
_____
_____
_____

Mark 2:10 (NIV)

[10] But I want you to know that the Son of Man has authority on earth to forgive sins."

Genesis 50:17, 20 (NIV)

[17] "This is what you are to say to Joseph: I ask you to forgive your brothers the sins and the wrongs they committed in treating you so badly.' Now please forgive the sins of the servants of the God of your father." When their message came to him, Joseph wept.

[20] You intended to harm me, but God intended it for good to accomplish what is now being done, the saving of many lives.

The Notebook

Matthew 6:14-15 (NIV)

[14] For if you forgive other people when they sin against you, your heavenly Father will also forgive you. [15] But if you do not forgive others their sins, your Father will not forgive your sins.

Is there anyone who you have not forgiven?
Why?
Do you realize that not forgiving is a sin?
Do you consider that it takes more effort to remain unforgiving than to forgive and heal?

_____
_____
_____
_____
_____
_____
_____
_____
_____
_____
_____
_____
_____
_____
_____

For the Christian Teen

How long have you had a religious or spiritual life? What faith or spiritual practices do you exercise? Why that faith?

_____
_____
_____
_____
_____
_____
_____
_____
_____
_____
_____
_____
_____
_____
_____

1 Thessalonians 4:5 (NIV)

[5] not in passionate lust like the pagans, who do not know God;

1 Corinthians 12:2 (NIV)

[2] You know that when you were pagans, somehow or other you were influenced and led astray to mute idols.

The Notebook

Psalm 35:1 (NIV)

¹ Contend, LORD, with those who contend with me;
  fight against those who fight against me.

Exodus 14:14 (NIV)

¹⁴ The LORD will fight for you; you need only to be still."

Deuteronomy 3:22 (NIV)

²² Do not be afraid of them; the LORD your God himself will fight for you."

Define conflict.
How do you resolve conflict with others?
Is your method healthy?

_____
_____
_____
_____
_____
_____
_____
_____
_____
_____
_____
_____
_____
_____
_____
_____
_____
_____

For the Christian Teen

How does God say we should handle authority?
Have you ever been in trouble/suspended from school?
What happened?
Did that consequence influence you to not do that again?

_____
_____
_____
_____
_____
_____
_____
_____
_____
_____
_____
_____
_____
_____

John 5:27 (NIV)

²⁷ And he has given him authority to judge because he is the Son of Man.

1 Peter 2:13-15 (NIV)

¹³ Submit yourselves for the Lord's sake to every human authority: whether to the emperor, as the supreme authority, ¹⁴ or to governors, who are sent by him to punish those who do wrong and to commend those who do right. ¹⁵ For it is God's will that by doing good you should silence the ignorant talk of foolish people.

The Notebook

1 Corinthians 6:19-20 (NIV)

[19] Do you not know that your bodies are temples of the Holy Spirit, who is in you, whom you have received from God? You are not your own; [20] you were bought at a price. Therefore honor God with your bodies.

What does the Bible say about the care of your body?
Have you ever been invited to try drugs?
Have you ever tried drugs? Do you want to try drugs?
Why?
How did it make you feel?
Why do you feel that you needed to try them?
Who did you share this experience with?
Do you know the long term and harmful effects of drug use?
Do you know of anyone addicted to drugs?
How would this contradict the body as a temple?

_____
_____
_____
_____
_____
_____
_____
_____
_____
_____
_____
_____
_____

For the Christian Teen

Ephesians 5:18 (NIV)

[18] Do not get drunk on wine, which leads to debauchery. Instead, be filled with the Spirit,

Have you ever been invited to try alcohol?
Have you ever tried alcohol?
Do you want to try alcohol?
Why?
How did it make you feel?
Why do you feel that you needed to try them?
Who did you share this experience with?
Do you know the long term and harmful effects of alcohol use?
Do you know of anyone addicted to alcohol?
Does God want to share your body with you while you are overindulging?

_____
_____
_____
_____
_____
_____
_____
_____
_____
_____
_____
_____

The Notebook

Matthew 26:41 (NIV)

⁴¹ "Watch and pray so that you will not fall into temptation. The spirit is willing, but the flesh is weak."

Have you ever been invited to try prescription drugs?
Have you ever tried prescription drugs?
Do you want to try prescription drugs?
Why?
How did it make you feel?
Why do you feel that you needed to try them?
Who did you share this experience with?
Do you know the long term and harmful effects of prescription drug use?
Do you know of anyone addicted to prescription drugs?
How would this contradict the body as a temple?

_____
_____
_____
_____
_____
_____
_____
_____
_____
_____
_____
_____
_____

For the Christian Teen

Define sex. What do you know? Where did you learn about sex?
Have you had sex?
How did you decide to have sex?
With whom did you have sex: someone special or someone random?
Why does God not want us to have sex before marriage?

_____
_____
_____
_____
_____
_____
_____
_____
_____
_____
_____
_____
_____
_____

Leviticus 21:13 (NIV)

[13] "The woman he marries must be a virgin.

1 Corinthians 7:9 (NIV)

[9] But if they cannot control themselves, they should marry, for it is better to marry than to burn with passion.

The Notebook

Matthew 4:1 (NIV)

Jesus Is Tested in the Wilderness

4 Then Jesus was led by the Spirit into the wilderness to be tempted[a] by the devil.

1 Corinthians 7:28 (NIV)

[28] But if you do marry, you have not sinned; and if a virgin marries, she has not sinned. But those who marry will face many troubles in this life, and I want to spare you this.

Do you want to have sex (if you have never)?
Why do you feel the need at this time to have sex?
Are you feeling pressured by your mate to have sex?
Do you feel comfortable and equipped to say no?
Do you know/understand that Jesus never had sex and lived for 33 years?

_____
_____
_____
_____
_____
_____
_____
_____
_____
_____
_____
_____
_____
_____
_____

For the Christian Teen

Do you send/receive nude/almost nude pictures of yourself and your peers?
Do you know that is considered child pornography?
Do you share the pictures you have been sent?
Has any of your nude "selfies" been shared?
How did you feel? Embarrassed?
What would Jesus say?
What would your parents say?

Ezekiel 16:30 (NIV)

[30] "'I am filled with fury against you,[a] declares the Sovereign LORD, when you do all these things, acting like a brazen prostitute!

_____
_____
_____
_____
_____
_____
_____
_____
_____
_____
_____
_____
_____
_____

The Notebook

Leviticus 18:10 (NIV)

¹⁰ "'Do not have sexual relations with your son's daughter or your daughter's daughter; that would dishonor you.

Have you ever been sexually abused, raped or molested?
Was it by someone you knew or trusted?
Who did you tell? Did the person you told believe you?
Do you know that God can heal you from that experience?
Do you want to be healed?
Do you know that God can help you forgive the person that did this to you?

_____
_____
_____
_____
_____
_____
_____
_____
_____
_____
_____
_____
_____
_____
_____

For the Christian Teen

What does God say about homosexuality?
Do you have any gay or lesbian friends?
How do you feel about the concept?
Have you ever wondered if that is a choice versus something natural?
Has anyone ever tried to persuade you to engage in the activities that define that label?
Did God create that?

_____
_____
_____
_____
_____
_____
_____
_____
_____
_____
_____
_____
_____

1 Timothy 1:9-10 (NIV)

[9] We also know that the law is made not for the righteous but for lawbreakers and rebels, the ungodly and sinful, the unholy and irreligious, for those who kill their fathers or mothers, for murderers, [10] for the sexually immoral, for those practicing homosexuality, for slave traders and liars and perjurers—and for whatever else is contrary to the sound doctrine

The Notebook

Psalm 139:14 (NIV)

¹⁴ I praise you because I am fearfully and wonderfully made;
   your works are wonderful,
   I know that full well.

Genesis 1:27 (NIV)

²⁷ So God created mankind in his own image,
   in the image of God he created them;
   male and female he created them.

Colossians 3:9-10 (NIV)

⁹ Do not lie to each other, since you have taken off your old self with its practices ¹⁰ and have put on the new self, which is being renewed in knowledge in the image of its Creator.

Define self-esteem.
Do you remember that God created you in His image?
Where would yours rate on a scale of 1 to 10?
What can you do to improve your self-esteem?
Who/what can help you to improve your self-esteem?
Why does God want you to have a healthy self-esteem?

_____
_____
_____
_____
_____
_____
_____
_____
_____
_____
_____
_____
_____
_____

Have you ever been physically abused by your guardian?
How do you feel about that?
Do you understand that God can equip you to forgive them?
Do you understand that God can heal you from that hurt and pain?

_____
_____
_____
_____
_____
_____
_____
_____
_____
_____
_____
_____
_____
_____

Leviticus 18:17 (NIV)

[17] "'Do not have sexual relations with both a woman and her daughter. Do not have sexual relations with either her son's daughter or her daughter's daughter; they are her close relatives. That is wickedness.

The Notebook

Genesis 2:17 (NIV)

¹⁷ but you must not eat from the tree of the knowledge of good and evil, for when you eat from it you will certainly die."

Deuteronomy 14:3 (NIV)

³ Do not eat any detestable thing.

What does God want you to eat?
Could you eat healthier?
What does God say about we take into our body?

_____
_____
_____
_____
_____
_____
_____
_____
_____
_____
_____
_____
_____
_____
_____
_____
_____

For the Christian Teen

Are you considered overweight?
What does God say about gluttony?
Why are you overeating?
What can you do to reduce that weight?
Is your weight affecting how you feel about yourself?
Is your weight affecting how others feel about you and treat you?

Luke 12:29-30 (NIV)

[29] And do not set your heart on what you will eat or drink; do not worry about it. [30] For the pagan world runs after all such things, and your Father knows that you need them.

_____
_____
_____
_____
_____
_____
_____
_____
_____
_____
_____
_____
_____
_____
_____

The Notebook

1 Samuel 27:1 (NIV)

David Among the Philistines

27 But David thought to himself, "One of these days I will be destroyed by the hand of Saul. The best thing I can do is to escape to the land of the Philistines. Then Saul will give up searching for me anywhere in Israel, and I will slip out of his hand."

Define bullying.
Have you ever been bullied?
Have you ever bullied someone?
What did you do to end the bullying?
Do you know that God is preparing you for war? Battle? Enemies?

_____
_____
_____
_____
_____
_____
_____
_____
_____
_____
_____
_____
_____
_____
_____

For the Christian Teen

Define friendship.
What are the characteristics of a friend?
Are you a great friend?
What can you do to be a better friend?
Do you know that Jesus is your friend?

_____
_____
_____
_____
_____
_____
_____
_____
_____
_____
_____
_____
_____

Proverbs 18:24 (NIV)

²⁴ One who has unreliable friends soon comes to ruin,
  but there is a friend who sticks closer than a brother.

Psalm 119:63 (NIV)

⁶³ I am a friend to all who fear you,
  to all who follow your precepts.

John 15:14 (NIV)

¹⁴ You are my friends if you do what I command.

The Notebook

John 12:8 (NIV)

⁸ "You will always have the poor among you,[a] but you will not always have me."

Ecclesiastes 3:1 (NIV)

A Time for Everything

3 There is a time for everything,
  and a season for every activity under the heavens:

What does God say about how we spend our time? Describe your best Saturday ever. Past or future.

_____
_____
_____
_____
_____
_____
_____
_____
_____
_____
_____
_____
_____
_____
_____
_____
_____

For the Christian Teen

What does God have planned for you?
What will you do beyond high school?
What makes that the best choice for you?
Who supports this choice? Why?
Who disagrees? Why?
How did you reach that decision?
Are you sharing what God does for you with others?

_____
_____
_____
_____
_____
_____
_____
_____
_____
_____
_____
_____
_____

Jeremiah 1:5 (NIV)

[5] "Before I formed you in the womb I knew[a] you,
  before you were born I set you apart;
  I appointed you as a prophet to the nations."

Jeremiah 29:11 (NIV)

[11] For I know the plans I have for you," declares the LORD, "plans to prosper you and not to harm you, plans to give you hope and a future.

The Notebook

John 14:13 (NIV)

¹³ And I will do whatever you ask in my name, so that the Father may be glorified in the Son.

Where does God want you to go to college?
What does God want you to study?
What does God want you to do with that study as a career?
Where would you like to attend college?
Who supports your decision?
What will be your major?
What else will you while there?

_____
_____
_____
_____
_____
_____
_____
_____
_____
_____
_____
_____
_____
_____
_____

For the Christian Teen

Do you trust God?
Does God trust you?
Who do you trust?
What do you trust them with?
Why?
What would have to happen to ruin your trust?

_____
_____
_____
_____
_____
_____
_____
_____
_____
_____
_____
_____
_____

Proverbs 3:5-6 (NIV)

[5] Trust in the LORD with all your heart
    and lean not on your own understanding;
[6] in all your ways submit to him,
    and he will make your paths straight.[

Psalm 25:1 (NIV)

[1] In you, LORD my God,
    I put my trust.

Psalm 33:21 (NIV)

[21] In him our hearts rejoice,
    for we trust in his holy name.

The Notebook

Psalm 119:15 (NIV)

¹⁵ I meditate on your precepts
 and consider your ways.

Psalm 1:5 (NIV)

⁵ Therefore the wicked will not stand in the judgment,
 nor sinners in the assembly of the righteous.

Psalm 19:14 (NIV)

¹⁴ May these words of my mouth and this meditation of my heart
 be pleasing in your sight,
 LORD, my Rock and my Redeemer.

How do you start your day?
How do you end the day?
How much time can you give God daily?
How will you spend time with God?

_____
_____
_____
_____
_____
_____
_____
_____
_____
_____
_____
_____
_____
_____
_____
_____
_____
_____

How do you spend time with God throughout the day?
How do you define a day as great or not?

_____
_____
_____
_____
_____
_____
_____
_____
_____
_____
_____
_____
_____
_____
_____
_____
_____

For the Christian Teen

1 Thessalonians 5:17 (NIV)

[17] pray continually

Psalm 119:164 (NIV)

[164] Seven times a day I praise you
   for your righteous laws.

Psalm 119:97 (NIV)

[97] Oh, how I love your law!
   I meditate on it all day long.

The Notebook

Ephesians 4:26-27 (NIV)

[26] "In your anger do not sin": Do not let the sun go down while you are still angry, [27] and do not give the devil a foothold.

How does God want us to handle our anger?
What do you do to calm down after being upset?
Who do you talk to about your issue? Adult? Peer?

_____
_____
_____
_____
_____
_____
_____
_____
_____
_____
_____
_____
_____
_____
_____
_____
_____
_____

For the Christian Teen

Are you involved in Fellowship of Christian Athletics or Christian school organizations?
What activities interest you at school?
Are you participating in those activities?
What does it take to be involved?

www.fca.org

_____
_____
_____
_____
_____
_____
_____
_____
_____
_____
_____
_____
_____
_____
_____

The Notebook

Luke 6:27-32 (NIV)

Love for Enemies

²⁷ "But to you who are listening I say: Love your enemies, do good to those who hate you, ²⁸ bless those who curse you, pray for those who mistreat you. ²⁹ If someone slaps you on one cheek, turn to them the other also. If someone takes your coat, do not withhold your shirt from them. ³⁰ Give to everyone who asks you, and if anyone takes what belongs to you, do not demand it back. ³¹ Do to others as you would have them do to you.

³² "If you love those who love you, what credit is that to you? Even sinners love those who love them.

Define enemies.
How do you identify your enemies?
How do you handle your enemies?
Do they know that you think of them as enemies?

_____
_____
_____
_____
_____
_____
_____
_____
_____
_____
_____
_____
_____
_____

For the Christian Teen

How do you measure another person's investment in your life?
How do you invite other's (teachers, parents, family, etc.) in your life?
How do you invest in the lives of others?
What does God say about investing in others?

_____
_____
_____
_____
_____
_____
_____
_____
_____
_____
_____
_____
_____
_____

1 Corinthians 1:4-6 (NIV)

Thanksgiving

⁴ I always thank my God for you because of his grace given you in Christ Jesus. ⁵ For in him you have been enriched in every way— with all kinds of speech and with all knowledge— ⁶ God thus confirming our testimony about Christ among you.

The Notebook

1 Timothy 1:5 (NIV)

⁵ The goal of this command is love, which comes from a pure heart and a good conscience and a sincere faith.

Hebrews 11:6 (NIV)

⁶ And without faith it is impossible to please God, because anyone who comes to him must believe that he exists and that he rewards those who earnestly seek him.

Ephesians 3:13 (NIV)

¹³ I ask you, therefore, not to be discouraged because of my sufferings for you, which are your glory.

What are your goals for your life?
Who knows these goals?
Who is helpful to hold you accountable for not quitting or keeping you from becoming discouraged?
Did God say that this was okay?

_____
_____
_____
_____
_____
_____
_____
_____
_____
_____
_____
_____
_____
_____
_____
_____

For the Christian Teen

What does God say about divorce?
How many of your friends have divorced parents?
Are your parents divorced?
How do you feel about divorce?
Have you asked God to heal your broken heart about being divorced?

_____
_____
_____
_____
_____
_____
_____
_____
_____
_____
_____
_____
_____
_____

Matthew 19:8-9 (NIV)

⁸ Jesus replied, "Moses permitted you to divorce your wives because your hearts were hard. But it was not this way from the beginning. ⁹ I tell you that anyone who divorces his wife, except for sexual immorality, and marries another woman commits adultery."

The Notebook

Ephesians 4:1-3 (NIV)

Unity and Maturity in the Body of Christ

4 As a prisoner for the Lord, then, I urge you to live a life worthy of the calling you have received. ² Be completely humble and gentle; be patient, bearing with one another in love. ³ Make every effort to keep the unity of the Spirit through the bond of peace.

Have you considered what God feels about your life?
What does God say about your personal life?
How do you feel about your life?
Why?

_____
_____
_____
_____
_____
_____
_____
_____
_____
_____
_____
_____
_____
_____
_____
_____
_____
_____

For the Christian Teen

Do you know anyone in foster care?
Do you know anyone who has been adopted?
How do you think they feel about being adopted?
How would you feel about being adopted?
What does God want us to do about those in need?
Would you help by adoption or foster parenting?

1 Samuel 1:28 (NIV)

²⁸ So now I give him to the LORD. For his whole life he will be given over to the LORD." And he worshiped the LORD there.

_____
_____
_____
_____
_____
_____
_____
_____
_____
_____
_____
_____
_____
_____

The Notebook

1 Corinthians 4:11 (NIV)

[11] To this very hour we go hungry and thirsty, we are in rags, we are brutally treated, we are homeless.

Do you know anyone who is homeless?
Have you and your family ever been homeless?
How do you feel about homelessness?
What does God charge us to do when people are homeless, hungry and otherwise in need?
What do you propose to do about homelessness?

_____
_____
_____
_____
_____
_____
_____
_____
_____
_____
_____
_____
_____
_____
_____
_____

For the Christian Teen

What do these verses mean to you?

_____
_____
_____
_____
_____
_____
_____
_____
_____
_____
_____
_____
_____
_____
_____
_____
_____
_____
_____
_____
_____
_____

Ephesians 3:14-21 (NIV)

[14] For this reason I kneel before the Father, [15] from whom every family[a] in heaven and on earth derives its name. [16] I pray that out of his glorious riches he may strengthen you with power through his Spirit in your inner being, [17] so that Christ may dwell in your hearts through faith. And I pray that you, being rooted and established in love, [18] may have power, together with all the Lord's holy people, to grasp how wide and long and high and deep is the love of Christ, [19] and to know this love that surpasses knowledge—that you may be filled to the measure of all the fullness of God.

[20] Now to him who is able to do immeasurably more than all we ask or imagine, according to his power that is at work within us, [21] to him be glory in the church and in Christ Jesus throughout all generations, for ever and ever! Amen.

Reflections

Reflections

Reflections

Appendix

Your Testimony	157
The Names of God	159
Prayer Directions	161
Prayer Request List/Journal	162
Favorite Scriptures	167
Goals	176
Mission	178
Vision	181
Values	185
Dreams	187

The Notebook

Your Testimony

Your testimony is your experience with God and the results of that experience. This includes your first encounter with Christ to your current life.

Consider the answers to the following questions to develop your testimony:
1. When did you first meet Christ?
2. How do you share how you met Christ with others?
3. What have your encounters with God been like?
4. What is your relationship with God like?
5. What has He kept you from?
6. What have you done that would have sabotaged God's work if He had not stopped you?
7. What has happened that you realized that only God was in charge to make this happen?

_____
_____
_____
_____
_____
_____
_____
_____
_____
_____
_____
_____
_____

The Notebook

The Names of God

(1) **_Elohim_**: The plural form of _EL_, meaning "strong one." It is used of false gods, but when used of the true God, it is a plural of majesty and intimates the trinity. It is especially used of God's sovereignty, creative work, mighty work for Israel and in relation to His sovereignty (Isa. 54:5; Jer. 32:27; Gen. 1:1; Isa. 45:18; Deut. 5:23; 8:15; Ps. 68:7).

Compounds of _El_:

- **_El Shaddai:_** "God Almighty." The derivation is uncertain. Some think it stresses God's loving supply and comfort; others His power as the Almighty one standing on a mountain and who corrects and chastens (Gen. 17:1; 28:3; 35:11; Ex. 6:1; Ps. 91:1, 2).
- **_El Elyon:_** "The Most High God." Stresses God's strength, sovereignty, and supremacy (Gen. 14:19; Ps. 9:2; Dan. 7:18, 22, 25).
- **_El Olam_**: "The Everlasting God." Emphasizes God's unchangeableness and is connected with His inexhaustibleness (Gen. 16:13).

(2) **_Yahweh (YHWH):_** Comes from a verb which means "to exist, be." This, plus its usage, shows that this name stresses God as the independent and self-existent God of revelation and redemption (Gen. 4:3; Ex. 6:3 (cf. 3:14); 3:12).

Compounds of _Yahweh_: Strictly speaking, these compounds are designations or titles which reveal additional facts about God's character.

- **_Yahweh Jireh (Yireh):_** "The Lord will provide." Stresses God's provision for His people (Gen. 22:14).
- **_Yahweh Nissi:_** "The Lord is my Banner." Stresses that God is our rallying point and our means of victory; the one who fights for His people (Ex. 17:15).
- **_Yahweh Shalom:_** "The Lord is Peace." Points to the Lord as the means of our peace and rest (Jud. 6:24).
- **_Yahweh Sabbaoth:_** "The Lord of Hosts." A military figure portraying the Lord as the commander of the armies of heaven (1 Sam. 1:3; 17:45).
- **_Yahweh Maccaddeshcem_**: "The Lord your Sanctifier." Portrays the Lord as our means of sanctification or as the one who sets believers apart for His purposes (Ex. 31:13).
- **_Yahweh Ro'i:_** "The Lord my Shepherd." Portrays the Lord as the Shepherd who cares for His people as a shepherd cares for the sheep of his pasture (Ps. 23:1).
- **_Yahweh Tsidkenu_**: "The Lord our Righteousness." Portrays the Lord as the means of our righteousness (Jer. 23:6).

- **Yahweh Shammah**: "The Lord is there." Portrays the Lord's personal presence in the millennial kingdom (Ezek. 48:35).
- **Yahweh Elohim Israel:** "The Lord, the God of Israel." Identifies Yahweh as the God of Israel in contrast to the false gods of the nations (Jud. 5:3.; Isa. 17:6).

(3) *Adonai:* Like *Elohim*, this too is a plural of majesty. The singular form means "master, owner." Stresses man's relationship to God as his master, authority, and provider (Gen. 18:2; 40:1; 1 Sam. 1:15; Ex. 21:1-6; Josh. 5:14).

(4) *Theos*: Greek word translated "God." Primary name for God used in the New Testament. Its use teaches: (1) *He is the only true God* (Matt. 23:9; Rom. 3:30); (2) *He is unique* (1 Tim. 1:17; John 17:3; Rev. 15:4; 16:7); (3) *He is transcendent* (Acts 17:24; Heb. 3:4; Rev. 10:6); (4) *He is the Savior* (John 3:16; 1 Tim. 1:1; 2:3; 4:10). This name is used of Christ as God in John 1:1, 18; 20:28; 1 John 5:20; Tit. 2:13; Rom. 9:5; Heb. 1:8; 2 Pet. 1:1.

(5) *Kurios*: Greek word translated "Lord." Stresses authority and supremacy. While it can mean sir (John 4:11), owner (Luke 19:33), master (Col. 3:22), or even refer to idols (1 Cor. 8:5) or husbands (1 Pet. 3:6), it is used mostly as the equivalent of *Yahweh* of the Old Testament. It too is used of Jesus Christ meaning (1) Rabbi or Sir (Matt. 8:6); (2) God or Deity (John 20:28; Acts 2:36; Rom. 10:9; Phil. 2:11).

(6) *Despotes*: Greek word translated "Master." Carries the idea of ownership while *kurios* stressed supreme authority (Luke 2:29; Acts 4:24; Rev. 6:10; 2 Pet. 2:1; Jude 4).

(7) *Father*: A distinctive New Testament revelation is that through faith in Christ, God becomes our personal Father. Father is used of God in the Old Testament only 15 times while it is used of God 245 times in the New Testament. As a name of God, it stresses God's loving care, provision, discipline, and the way we are to address God in prayer (Matt. 7:11; Jam. 1:17; Heb. 12:5-11; John 15:16; 16:23; Eph. 2:18; 3:15; 1 Thess. 3:11).

Source: http://www.agapebiblestudy.com/documents/the%20many%20names%20of%20god.htm

For the Christian Teen

Prayer
A Short How To Guide

The prayers which are most effective follow the following "rules:"

- It is a conversation with God.
- Be Honest with God.
- This is a relationship.
- God is to be praised, worshiped and glorified.
- God likes His word prayed back to Him.
- This is not a list of stuff you want.
- Think of more than yourself when you pray.
- Be authentic with God and yourself.
- Be prepared for people to ask you about your prayer life and faith.
- Do not worry about big words or long sentences.
- Please know that God is not taking revenge on others for you, and vice versa.
- Please prayer in the name of Jesus.
- There is no correct way to pray.

Scriptures on Prayer

Matthew 6:9-14

1 Thessalonians 5:17

Matthew 26:

John 17

The Notebook

Prayer Requests
Prayer Journal

1. What are you asking God for?
2. What are you hoping God will do?
3. What are you expecting from God?
4. What has God already done to exceed your expectations?
5. What has God done to get your attention?
6. What has He shown about Himself and you?

_____
_____
_____
_____
_____
_____
_____
_____
_____
_____
_____
_____
_____
_____

For the Christian Teen

The Notebook

The Notebook

For the Christian Teen

Favorite Scriptures

Numbers 6:24-26

[24] The LORD bless you and keep you;
[25] the LORD make his face shine on you and be gracious to you;
[26] the LORD turn his face toward you and give you peace."

Jeremiah 1:5

[5] "Before I formed you in the womb I knew[a] you, before you were born I set you apart; I appointed you as a prophet to the nations."

Jeremiah 29:11

[11] For I know the plans I have for you," declares the LORD, "plans to prosper you and not to harm you, plans to give you hope and a future.

Psalm 1

[1] Blessed is the one
who does not walk in step with the wicked
or stand in the way that sinners take
or sit in the company of mockers,
[2] but whose delight is in the law of the LORD,
and who meditates on his law day and night.
[3] That person is like a tree planted by streams of water,
which yields its fruit in season
and whose leaf does not wither—
whatever they do prospers.

[4] Not so the wicked!
They are like chaff

that the wind blows away.
⁵ Therefore the wicked will not stand in the judgment,
nor sinners in the assembly of the righteous.

⁶ For the LORD watches over the way of the righteous,
but the way of the wicked leads to destruction.

Psalm 8

¹ LORD, our Lord,
how majestic is your name in all the earth!

You have set your glory
in the heavens.
² Through the praise of children and infants
you have established a stronghold against your enemies,
to silence the foe and the avenger.
³ When I consider your heavens,
the work of your fingers,
the moon and the stars,
which you have set in place,
⁴ what is mankind that you are mindful of them,
human beings that you care for them?[c]

⁵ You have made them[d] a little lower than the angels[e]
and crowned them[f] with glory and honor.
⁶ You made them rulers over the works of your hands;
you put everything under their[g] feet:
⁷ all flocks and herds,
and the animals of the wild,
⁸ the birds in the sky,
and the fish in the sea,
all that swim the paths of the seas.

⁹ LORD, our Lord,
how majestic is your name in all the earth!

Psalm 19:14

[14] May these words of my mouth and this meditation of my heart be pleasing in your sight, LORD, my Rock and my Redeemer.

Psalm 23 (KJV)

[1] The LORD is my shepherd; I shall not want.

[2] He maketh me to lie down in green pastures: he leadeth me beside the still waters.

[3] He restoreth my soul: he leadeth me in the paths of righteousness for his name's sake.

[4] Yea, though I walk through the valley of the shadow of death, I will fear no evil: for thou art with me; thy rod and thy staff they comfort me.

[5] Thou preparest a table before me in the presence of mine enemies: thou anointest my head with oil; my cup runneth over.

[6] Surely goodness and mercy shall follow me all the days of my life: and I will dwell in the house of the LORD forever.

Psalm 46:1

[1] God is our refuge and strength,
an ever-present help in trouble.

Psalm 46:10

[10] "Be still, and know that I am God;
I will be exalted among the nations,
I will be exalted in the earth."

Psalm 100

The Notebook

[1] Shout for joy to the LORD, all the earth.
[2] Worship the LORD with gladness;
come before him with joyful songs.
[3] Know that the LORD is God.
It is he who made us, and we are his[a];
we are his people, the sheep of his pasture.

[4] Enter his gates with thanksgiving
and his courts with praise;
give thanks to him and praise his name.
[5] For the LORD is good and his love endures forever;
his faithfulness continues through all generations.

Psalm 119:11

[11] I have hidden your word in my heart that I might not sin against you.

Psalm 139:14

[14] I praise you because I am fearfully and wonderfully made; your works are wonderful, I know that full well.

Proverbs 3:5-6

[5] Trust in the LORD with all your heart and lean not on your own understanding;
[6] in all your ways acknowledge him, and he will make your paths straight.

Proverbs 23:7 (KJV)

[7] For as he thinketh in his heart, so is he: Eat and drink, saith he to thee; but his heart is not with thee.

Habakkuk 2:2

[2] Then the LORD replied:

"Write down the revelation
and make it plain on tablets
so that a herald[a] may run with it.

Matthew 11:28, 30

[28] "Come to me, all you who are weary and heavy-ladened, and I will give you rest.

[30] For my yoke is easy and my burden is light."

Matthew 14:31

[31] Immediately Jesus reached out his hand and caught him. "You of little faith," he said, "why did you doubt?"

Matthew 22:37

[37] Jesus replied: "'Love the Lord your God with all your heart and with all your soul and with all your mind.

Matthew 28:19-20

[19] Therefore go and make disciples of all nations, baptizing them in[a] the name of the Father and of the Son and of the Holy Spirit, [20] and teaching them to obey everything I have commanded you. And surely I am with you always, to the very end of the age."

Luke 9:23-24

[23] Then he said to them all: "If anyone would come after me, he must deny himself and take up his cross daily and follow me. [24] For whoever wants to save his life will lose it, but whoever loses his life for me will save it.

Luke 23:34

The Notebook

[34] Jesus said, "Father, forgive them, for they do not know what they are doing."[a] And they divided up his clothes by casting lots.

John 1:1-2

[1] In the beginning was the Word, and the Word was with God, and the Word was God. [2] He was with God in the beginning.

John 3:16

[16] "For God so loved the world that he gave his one and only Son,[a] that whoever believes in him shall not perish but have eternal life.

John 3:30

[30] He must become greater; I must become less.

John 11:35

[35] Jesus wept.

Romans 8:26

[26] In the same way, the Spirit helps us in our weakness. We do not know what we ought to pray for, but the Spirit himself intercedes for us with groans that words cannot express.

1 Corinthians 10:13

[13] No temptation has seized you except what is common to man. And God is faithful; he will not let you be tempted beyond what you can bear. But when you are tempted, he will also provide a way out so that you can stand up under it.

Galatians 5:22-23

[22] But the fruit of the Spirit is love, joy, peace, patience, kindness, goodness, faithfulness, [23] gentleness and self-control. Against such things there is no law.

Ephesians 3:14-21

[14] For this reason I kneel before the Father, [15] from whom his whole family[a] in heaven and on earth derives its name. [16] I pray that out of his glorious riches he may strengthen you with power through his Spirit in your inner being, [17] so that Christ may dwell in your hearts through faith. And I pray that you, being rooted and established in love, [18] may have power, together with all the saints, to grasp how wide and long and high and deep is the love of Christ, [19] and to know this love that surpasses knowledge—that you may be filled to the measure of all the fullness of God.

[20] Now to him who is able to do immeasurably more than all we ask or imagine, according to his power that is at work within us, [21] to him be glory in the church and in Christ Jesus throughout all generations, for ever and ever! Amen.

Ephesians 4:26-27

[26] "In your anger do not sin"[a]: Do not let the sun go down while you are still angry, [27] and do not give the devil a foothold.

Ephesians 4:32

[32] Be kind and compassionate to one another, forgiving each other, just as in Christ God forgave you.

Philippians 4:7

[7] And the peace of God, which transcends all understanding, will guard your hearts and your minds in Christ Jesus.

Philippians 4:13-17

[13] I can do everything through him who gives me strength.

The Notebook

¹⁴ Yet it was good of you to share in my troubles. ¹⁵ Moreover, as you Philippians know, in the early days of your acquaintance with the gospel, when I set out from Macedonia, not one church shared with me in the matter of giving and receiving, except you only; ¹⁶ for even when I was in Thessalonica, you sent me aid again and again when I was in need. ¹⁷ Not that I am looking for a gift, but I am looking for what may be credited to your account.

Colossians 3:23

²³ Whatever you do, work at it with all your heart, as working for the Lord, not for men,

1 Thessalonians 5:17

¹⁷ pray continually;

Hebrews 11:6

⁶ And without faith it is impossible to please God, because anyone who comes to him must believe that he exists and that he rewards those who earnestly seek him.

Hebrews 13:5b

⁵ Keep your lives free from the love of money and be content with what you have, because God has said,

"Never will I leave you;
never will I forsake you."

James 1:2-5

² Consider it pure joy, my brothers, whenever you face trials of many kinds, ³ because you know that the testing of your faith develops perseverance. ⁴ Perseverance must finish its work so that you may be mature and complete, not lacking anything. ⁵ If any of you lacks wisdom, he should ask God, who gives generously to all without finding fault, and it will be given to him.

Jude 24

²⁴Now unto him that is able to keep you from falling, and to present you faultless before the presence of his glory with exceeding joy,

Revelation 3:16

¹⁶ So, because you are lukewarm—neither hot nor cold—I am about to spit you out of my mouth.

The Notebook

Goals

goal [gohl] *noun*

the result or achievement toward <u>which</u> effort is directed; aim; end.

The questions that you answer when developing goals are as follows:

1. What do I want to accomplish for God, with God, because of God?
2. When do I want to accomplish this by? What does God's timing look like?
3. Who is going to help me and hold me accountable? Who has God sent my way for this matter?
4. What do you do when you do not meet the goals as planned? What will God do in the meantime?
5. Who do you share your successes with? How will God use my achievement to help others?

For the Christian Teen

Goals

Goals	By When	Who

The Notebook

Mission Statement

A personal mission statement is based on habit 2 of 7 Habits of Highly Effective People called begin with the end in mind. In ones life, the most effective way to begin with the end in mind is to develop a mission statement one that focuses what you want to be in terms of character and what you want to do in reference to contribution of achievements. Writing a mission statement can be the most important activity an individual can take to truly lead ones life.

Victor Hugo once said there is nothing as powerful as an idea whose time has finally come, you may call it a credo, a philosophy, you may call it a purpose statement, it's not as important as to what you call it, no it's how you define your definition. That mission and vision statement is more powerful, more significant, more influential, than the baggage of the past, or even the accumulated noise of the present.

What is a mission statement you ask? Personal mission statements based on correct principles are like a personal constitution, the basis for making major, life-directing decisions, the basis for making daily decisions in the midst of the circumstances and emotions that affect our lives.

Your statement may be a few words or several pages, but it is not a "to do" list. It reflects your uniqueness and must speak to you powerfully about the person you are and the person you are becoming.

Why should you write a personal mission statement?

Numerous experts on leadership and personal development emphasize how vital it is for you to craft your own personal vision for your life. Warren Bennis, Stephen Covey, Peter Senge, and others point out that a powerful vision can help you succeed far beyond where you'd be without one. That vision can propel you and inspire those around you to reach their own dreams.

Q: How do I go about creating my Personal Mission Statement?

A: A Mission Statement is defined as having goals and a deadline. This is opposed to the notion that a Mission Statement is just a bunch of flowery, general phrases like, "I will be the best business person I can be."

What should you include when writing a great personal mission statement?

- describe your best characteristics and how you express them
- have specific, measurable outcomes (or goals)
- have a deadline — for example, December 31st 2012, or a year from today.

When Stephen Covey talks about 'mission statement' in this quote, he is referring to the articulation of your life purpose. "If you don't set your goals based upon your Mission Statement, you may be climbing the ladder of success only to realize, when you get to the top, you're on the WRONG BUILDING." **Stephen Covey – 7 Habits of Highly Effective People.**

Mission Statement Example – Poor (It's more like a Vision Statement)

"I aspire to start my own business. I want to help others and be a better businesswoman. I will deliver the best food with the highest service levels." Jane

Mission Statement Example – Better

"I will start my business within 3 months and plan to grow it to $500,000 in revenues within a year. Using this success, my staff and I will spread the word to local schools and businesses about eco-friendly food production in order that we reach at least 100 people within the same time frame. My purpose will be to massively add value to our local community in measurable ways that have a real impact on people's health now and in the future," Jane.

What to do with your Mission Statement?

So now we have a mission, we can set a range of goals on the road to achieving your outcomes and dreams. Your values are clarified and should be in line with the goals you want to achieve in life so you should find it easier to make decisions and to do the "right thing" because you can simply ask yourself, "Will this help me achieve my mission?"

You can even put your mission statement in an area where your family or even co-workers will see it. For, a mission statement defines who you are and what you stand for. This lets people see how you think and feel, which in turn, will help them respect, think and act in line with your values too.

Mission Statement

For the Christian Teen

Vision Statement

A personal vision/mission statement is the framework for creating a powerful life.

Your personal vision statement provides the direction necessary to guide the course of your days and the choices you make about your life.

The idea is to craft a broad based idea about your life and what will really make it exciting and fulfilling, that's your life vision.

From the vision, you craft a more focused and action orientated "mission" statement based on "purpose." And finally you get to a list of goals, wishes, desires and needs.

In his book 'The Success Principles,' Jack Canfield tells us that in order to create a balanced and successful life; your vision needs to include the following seven areas:

1. work and career
2. finances
3. recreation and free time
4. health and fitness
5. relationships
6. personal goals
7. contribution to the larger community

It does not include the distinctive ways that you intend to accomplish your purpose.

Why Write a Personal Vision Statement?

To express:

- your purpose
- your life's dream
- your core values & beliefs
- what you want for yourself

The Notebook

- what you want to contribute to others
- what you want to be

Characteristics of a Vision Statement:

- Engages your heart & spirit
- Taps into embedded concerns & needs
- Asserts what you want to create
- Is something worth going for
- Provides meaning to the work you do
- Is a little cloudy and grand
- Is simple
- Is a living document
- Provides a starting place from which to get more specificity
- Is based on quality and dedication

Key Elements of a Vision Statement:

- Written down and referred to daily
- Written in present tense, as if it has already been completed
- Includes a variety of activities and time frames
- Filled with descriptive details that anchor it to reality

What Visions Are Not:

- A mission statement: "Why do we exist now?"
- A strategic plan: "How do we plan to get there?"
- A set of objectives: "We will accomplish X by Y time to Z% target audience."

Use these questions to guide your thoughts:

- What are the ten things you most enjoy doing? Be honest. These are the ten things without which your weeks, months, and years would feel incomplete.
- What three things must you do every single day to feel fulfilled in your work?
- What are your five-six most important values?

- Your life has a number of important facets or dimensions, all of which deserve some attention in your personal vision statement.
- Write one important goal for each of them: physical, spiritual, work or career, family, social relationships, financial security, mental improvement and attention, and fun.
- If you never had to work another day in your life, how would you spend your time instead of working?
- When your life is ending, what will you regret not doing, seeing, or achieving?
- What strengths have other people commented on about you and your accomplishments? What strengths do you see in yourself?

Vision Statement

For the Christian Teen

Values Statement

A personal **value** is absolute or relative and ethical value, the assumption of which can be the basis for ethical action. A *value system* is a set of consistent values and measures. A *principle value* is a foundation upon which other values and measures of integrity are based.

Some values are physiologically determined and are normally considered objective, such as a desire to avoid physical pain or to seek pleasure. Other values are considered subjective, vary across individuals and cultures, and are in many ways aligned with belief and belief systems. Types of values include ethical/moral values, doctrinal/ideological (religious, political) values, social values, and aesthetic values. It is debated whether some values that are not clearly physiologically determined, such as altruism, are intrinsic, and whether some, such as acquisitiveness, should be classified as vices or virtues. Values have been studied in various disciplines: anthropology, behavioral economics, business ethics, corporate governance, moral philosophy, political sciences, social psychology, sociology and theology to name a few.

Values can be defined as broad preference concerning appropriate courses of action or outcomes. As such, values reflect a person's sense of right and wrong or what "ought" to be. "Equal rights for all", "Excellence deserves admiration", and "People should be treated with respect and dignity" are representative of values. Values tend to influence attitudes and behavior.

Values Statement

Dreams List

The Notebook

The Notebook

Resources

www.onediagage.com
www.forchristianteens.com
www.lifeway.com
www.fervr.net
www.christianitytoday.com/iyf
christianteens.about.com
http://higherpraise.com/
http://www.projectinspired.com/
http://christiananswers.net/teens/home.html
http://www.usa.gov/Topics/Teens.shtml
http://www.teenink.com/Resources
http://www.parentandteenresources.com/
http://www.hhs.gov/ash/oah/oah-initiatives/teen_pregnancy/
http://www.cdc.gov/teenpregnancy/parents.htm
www.thenationalcampaign.org/resources/
http://www.suicidepreventionlifeline.org/
http://www.drugfree.org/
http://kidshealth.org/teen/food_fitness/dieting/obesity.html
http://www.medicalnewstoday.com/articles/268983.php
http://www.jhsph.edu/research/centers-and-institutes/center-for-adolescent-health/_includes/Obesity_Standalone.pdf

The Notebook

192 | Minister Onedia and Hillary

Acknowledgements

God, thank You for Your plans for me. Thank You for *The Notebook For the Christian Teen,* and choosing me to complete Your project. I just want to please You, God. Thank You for continuing to anoint me and to invest in me and my gifts, which keep surprising me. Thank You for loving and forgiving me.

Hillary and Nehemiah, thank you for supporting me and my endeavors. Thank you for loving me, especially when I do nothing without a pen and a clipboard, thank you for enduring my late nights, your ideas, the sounding board, the love and the support. Thank you for celebrating our legacy.

To my co-author: Hillary Nicole. Thank you for journeying with me on this endeavor. I hope that you are proud of your legacy. This was an unexpected gift and God keeps doing it over and over again. Hosanna!

To our reading team: Kim Joiner and Willie Jackson. Thank you for reading and answering the questions and editing those errors and clarifying those unclear areas. Your time, effort and contribution means a lot to me.

To my prayer partners and to my accountability partners, thank you for the long talks and the powerful prayers and the encouragement.

To the readers who this will reach and empower and touch and affect, may these words empower you and help you reach some resolve. May you be inspired to achieve your goals and dreams. May you enhance your relationship with God so that your other relationships will also improve. May you enhance your self-esteem through prayer and study. May you have courage and peace. Share love the best you can until you can share love without reservation.

The Notebook

For the Christian Teen

About the Inquisitive Ones

The author of these questions was an inquisitive child. And now an adult of the same nature. She seeks to ask you so that you grow and are challenged appropriately.
Hillary asks lots of questions too. And holds us accountable for her answers!
Do not hesitate to ask them!
@onediangage (twitter) * onediagage@onediagage.com * facebook.com/onediagageministries
youtube.com/onediagage * blogtalkradio.com/onediagage * ongage (instagram) * lsu_all_day_ (instagram)
www.onediagage.com

The Notebook

For the Christian Teen

PREACHER ♦ TEACHER ♦ FACILITATOR
CONFERENCE SPEAKER ♦ PANELIST ♦ WORKSHOP LEADER

To invite Ms. Gage to speak at your church, youth group, or youth ministry,
Please contact us at: www.onedigage.com
@onediangage (twitter) ♦ onediagage@onediagage.com ♦ facebook.com/onediagageministries
youtube.com/onediagage ♦ blogtalkradio.com/onediagage

The Notebook

For the Christian Teen

Publishing

Do you have a book you want to write, but do not know what to do?
Do you have a book you need to publish but do not know how to start?
Would publishing move your career forward?

Let us help

onediagage@purpleink.net ♦ www.purpleink.net

713.705.5530 ♦ 512.715.4243

www.ingramcontent.com/pod-product-compliance
Lightning Source LLC
Chambersburg PA
CBHW080450170426
43196CB00016B/2747